Space

priddy books
big ideas for little people

The Universe is mind-bogglingly big.
It is everything that exists—
every speck of dust, rock, planet,
solar system, and galaxy.

It is difficult to imagine how big
the Universe is because we think
it's infinite (never-ending),
containing an unimaginable
number of stars!

This is a nebula,
where new stars
and galaxies
are made.

This huge cosmic
pillar is made
of hydrogen
and dust.

The Universe

The Milky Way

Galaxies come in all different shapes. This one is a spiral.

A black hole is thought to exist in the middle.

We are somewhere here!

The Milky Way is one of the billions of galaxies that exist in the known Universe, and it is also home to our solar system. It is called a spiral galaxy due to its shape, and contains between 200 and 400 billion stars (like the Sun), and some 100 billion planets!

The Sun

Mercury

The closest
to the Sun

The asteroid belt
is between Mars
and Jupiter.

The perfect
conditions
for life

Venus

Earth

The hottest
planet

Mars

Has a volcano
bigger than
Mount Everest

The solar system is where
we call home. The Sun is in the
middle of the solar system,
and everything else orbits around it.

There are a total of eight planets,
some with their own moons, as well as
five dwarf planets, including Pluto.
Earth is the third planet closest to the Sun.

The Solar System

Jupiter

The biggest planet

Uranus

Has 27 moons

Saturn

Rings of ice and dust

Winds blow at 1,500 mph

Neptune

Up until 2006, there were nine planets in our solar system, but scientists took away Pluto's planet status. It is now a minor planet, or dwarf planet. Poor Pluto!

Smaller than some moons in the solar system, Mercury is the planet closest to the Sun.

It looks very similar to the surface of our moon, and is covered in craters made when huge asteroids crashed into its surface.

Mercury is so dense, it has a large core made of pure molten iron!

The side of Mercury that faces the Sun is up to 10 times hotter than Earth.

Mercury has one of the largest impact craters in the solar system.

Mercury

Venus

It is sometimes called Earth's "sister planet."

Venus is the brightest planet in our skies.

It was once thought that Venus was similar to Earth, and that life might even exist there, but we were very wrong.

In fact, it is the most unfriendly planet in the solar system! Its surface temperature is so hot, it could melt lead; its air is mainly composed of carbon dioxide; and there are layers of poisonous sulphuric acid clouds in its atmosphere.

Its diameter is only 400 miles less than that of Earth's.

Key facts:
Order from the Sun: 2nd
Size: Nearly the same size as Earth
Number of moons: 0
Type: Terrestrial planet

Earth

Earth is the only known planet in our solar system with life. We call Earth the Blue Planet because of the oceans that cover most of the surface. The Earth takes 24 hours to rotate on its axis, giving us day and night, and 365 days to orbit the Sun, giving us changes in seasons.

The Moon orbits Earth.

The ozone layer protects us from the Sun's harmful rays.

Oceans cover 70 percent of Earth's surface.

Key facts:
Order from the Sun: 3rd
Size: 5th largest
Number of moons: 1
Type: Terrestrial planet

Mars

Mars' red shade is made by iron in the planet's surface.

Mars is known as the Red Planet. It is the planet that is most like Earth, but it is very cold because it is farther from the Sun.

Scientists have discovered ice beneath its surface. This may mean that life once existed there!

Huge craters, valleys, and mountains cover the surface.

Across the middle is Valles Marineris, a canyon nine times the length of the Grand Canyon.

Key facts:
Order from the Sun: 4th
Size: Half Earth's size
Number of moons: 2
Type: Terrestrial planet

On November 13, 1971, Mariner 9 became the first space probe to maintain orbit around another planet, and this was Mars! Exciting pictures and data were beamed back down to Earth.

Jupiter

Jupiter is the biggest planet in our solar system. It is 2.5 times the size of all the other planets combined!

It is made mainly from gas and is known as one of the four gas giants along with Saturn, Uranus, and Neptune.

The planet is covered in thick red, brown, yellow, and white clouds.

The Great Red Spot is a huge storm three times the size of Earth.

Jupiter is a very stormy planet with winds of more than 400 mph.

Jupiter's four largest moons

Io   Europa   Ganymede   Callisto

Saturn is the second-largest planet in the solar system.
It has nine beautiful rings that can be seen with a telescope.
They are made up of ice, rock, and dust. Saturn spins very
fast on its axis—a day on Saturn lasts only 10 hours.

Some ring particles are dust-sized,
while some are as big as mountains.
They are made from comets, asteroids,
or shattered moons.

Saturn

Key facts:
Order from the Sun: 6th
Size: 764 Earths
Number of moons: 62
Type: Gas giant

ROTATION DIRECTION

Uranus is so far away, if you were traveling there from the Sun and you made it to Saturn, you'd only be halfway there!

It is very cold here with temperatures reaching as low as -371°F above its cloud layer. Little is known about this distant, blue planet.

Uranus is the only planet that rotates on its side.

The bright blue color comes from methane gas.

Uranus

Neptune

Voyager 2 is the first and only spacecraft to pass this distant planet.

The farthest planet out from the Sun, Neptune is a cold, icy giant. It is a bright blue, due to methane gas, with a water layer that leads down to a solid core the size of Earth.

Neptune takes 165 years to orbit the Sun, meaning that its winter lasts for 40 years!

The Great Dark Spot is a storm the size of planet Earth.

Its orbit of the Sun takes so long that it has only been around the Sun once since its discovery in 1846.

Key facts:
Order from the Sun: 8th
Size: 57 Earths
Number of moons: 13
Type: Gas giant

People who watch the skies are called astronomers. They use telescopes to study the sky and look at planets, stars, and galaxies, and cosmic events such as supernovas.

People have been looking at the stars for thousands of years. It is impossible to imagine just how many stars there are in the Universe.

This is the Big Dipper constellation.

Many important space discoveries have been made by people using telescopes.

Stars

The Sun

The Sun is the star at the middle of our solar system. It gives us heat and light for life on Earth.

It is a giant burning ball of hydrogen and helium gas, with a surface temperature of 9,932°F. That's HOT!

The energy from the Sun is called the solar wind.

Red areas of the Sun are the coolest.

Sudden huge explosions of energy are called solar flares.

The Moon

The Moon is a dry, dusty place with no air. It is covered in hollows called craters, made by huge meteoroids crashing into its surface, which still happens today! Ocean tides on Earth are caused by the Moon's gravitational force.

The Moon is the only place in space where humans have landed.

The Moon takes 27 days, 7 hours, 43 minutes, 11.6 seconds to orbit Earth.

The Moon's surface is covered in impact craters.

In 1969, the American astronaut Neil Armstrong became the first man to walk on the Moon. His footprints from 1969 can still be seen on the Moon's surface today.

Apollo Lunar Module carried a crew of two from lunar orbit to the Moon's surface and back.

The Moon is an incredible 4.5 billion years old.

Rockets

Every space mission begins at mission control, where a team of scientists and engineers prepare to launch a rocket into space. Huge rockets are ignited on a launch pad. The rockets gain enough power to take off, rise up, and enter space, climbing over 1,000 feet in a few seconds.

This Apollo rocket had a crew of three, seated in the top.

The biggest rocket to date was Saturn V, at over 360 feet.

Mission Control

Rocket missions are controlled from Earth at mission control. Teams of scientists, engineers, and flight controllers track a rocket's progress from the point of liftoff.

Rockets are so powerful, they shoot up high into the atmosphere.

Astronauts

Astronauts are brave men and women who venture into space. They are sent on special missions. Some astronauts have landed on the Moon, while others are sent to work on space stations orbiting the Earth.

Oxygen supply tank

Protective helmet

The astronaut is out on a space walk.

Key facts:

First in space:
Yuri Gagarin

First on the Moon:
Neil Armstrong

Fastest speed traveled:
Apollo 10 astronauts,
6.88 miles per second

Most time spent in space:
Gennady Padalka, almost 2.5 years

Longest single stay in space:
Valeri Polyakov, 438 days

Space Tourism

How about a trip into space for your next vacation? It's very possible, with companies like Virgin Galactic developing new spacecraft to do so. Scientists hope that one day we might be able to use the same spacecraft to travel across the world in just three hours!

Ticket to fly

Tickets for the first Virgin Galactic flight are on sale now, for US $250,000.

Passengers will experience zero gravity.